Haym Salomon

HAYM

The Jewish Publication Society

Philadelphia / New York / Jerusalem

Shirley Milgrim

SALOMON

Liberty's Son

illustrated by RICHARD FISH

Copyright ©1979 by The Jewish Publication Society
First paperback edition   All rights reserved
ISBN 0–8276–0073–9
      0–8276–0256–1 (pbk)
Library of Congress catalog card number 75–17349
Manufactured in the United States of America
Designed by Adrianne Onderdonk Dudden

Haym Salomon

An August sun simmered on the horizon. And though the hour was well past seven in the evening, heat waves continued to rise from the peaked roofs of the Dutch houses on Manhattan Island. To Haym Salomon, trudging toward the limits of the city of New York, his feet baking in his boots, sweat trickling down his bony neck, this summer of 1778 seemed the hottest in all his thirty-eight years. He squinted into the blood-red sun and longed for night.

To the passerby, the black-clad man walking along the road scarcely merited a second glance—a valuable asset for an agent of the Sons of Liberty, the American revolutionaries who were outlawed in British-occupied New York. This was Haym's fifth mission for them. So far he'd been lucky. He had helped American captives escape from the fearful Provost Prison under the noses of the British military police. He'd even convinced Hessian mercenaries, who had been hired by the British to fight for them, to desert and come over to the side of the Colonies—and he was still free to tell the tale.

But Haym couldn't help but wonder, as the sun bit into the waters of the Hudson River, if his good luck would fail him tonight. He continued to stride forward, however—a slight, solitary figure on the country lane whose footsteps scarcely disturbed the dust.

Haym turned over tonight's plan in his mind. He had worked out the scheme with Isaac Sears, leader of the "Liberty Boys" in New York. Haym would meet a Scot named John McClay at the old windmill a mile and a half up Manhattan Island. He would borrow McClay's horse and wagon, which he needed to carry a wounded American soldier, hiding in the Salomon cellar, out of town. The soldier boy would be hidden in the wagon and brought back to the mill. Then McClay would deliver him to the encampment of the Continental army at Dobbs Ferry.

A simple plan. But Haym could not quiet his thumping heart. The Salomon house stood in the heart of town near the wharves, where inquisitive eyes peered from every window. Moreover, there was only one city street that wasn't blocked by rubble from a fire set by the British a few days earlier. That street was Broad Way. He would have to drive the clumsy farm wagon right past the British prison and, farther on, the British barracks!

He sighed deeply. An acrid smell made him cough. The fire had burned down five hundred buildings and the smoke lingered on. But soon pure country air soothed Haym Salomon's lungs, and his smarting eyes rested on a field of daisies and a roadside cottage, purple in the twilight. Two farmers sat in front of the cottage gossiping.

"I don't see," said one, drawing on his long-stemmed clay pipe, "that the Virginian is much of a general. Always getting licked! Lost the Battle of Long Island, didn't he?"

"And now New York ruined by fire," added the second. "The British say 'twas an accident, but I don't believe it!"

"What will the Sons of Liberty do now, I wonder?"

The men fell silent as Salomon approached.

"Evening," he said.

They replied, "Evening," and their eyes followed him until he was well up the road.

For an underground organization, Haym thought, the Sons of Liberty made a lot of noise. He counted on his fingers the ways they openly harassed the enemy. One, they spoke out at town meetings; two, they publicly humiliated unpopular officials by demanding that they come before the people to explain their behavior or be tarred and feathered; three, they threatened British officers and their families; four, they made martyrs of every patriot who met death violently (even if it was in a street brawl). Other chapters of the Sons of Liberty might boast of such fiery orators as Boston's Sam Adams or Virginia's Patrick Henry. But New York's glory lay in their great numbers. There were more "Freedom Boys" in New York than in any other occupied city.

Ironic, Haym thought, that not one of these rebel Americans, with all their noble slogans, had ever known real oppression—at least not the kind that he had experienced. As a Jew born and reared in Poland —a land where Jews had lived for hundreds of years but were still not welcome—Salomon learned at an early age about restriction, humiliation, and tyranny. "Give me liberty or give me death!" the American patriot Patrick Henry had proclaimed in response to British provocations. How might he or Thomas Paine have reacted to the crushing oppression suffered by Jews of Russia and Poland?

Lissa, where Haym was born, was put to the torch in 1767. The Jews of the town faced a bleak future, and the twenty-seven-year-old Haym Salomon set out to seek his fortune in the few tolerant capitals of Europe: Berlin, Paris, London, where fellow Jews had settled and established businesses. Fluent in languages, he already knew Russian, German, and Polish as well as his native Yiddish. As he moved across Europe he learned French, Italian, and English. The Jewish merchants who took Salomon in and taught him their business never regretted it. He was industrious and honest.

They showed him how to buy merchandise fresh off the ships and sell it at a commission, and how to handle the exchange of money from one country to another.

But Haym was not content in the Old World. Everywhere, even in the great capitals, he saw that Jews suffered from prejudice. One day his employer showed him a letter written in Yiddish from a relative in New York:

Here we can bring up our children as Jews. We have a synagogue, a person to kill meat according to ritual, a Hebrew teacher. We are all doing business in this city of 20,000 people. Our community flourishes. No one stops us from fighting alongside Americans of every creed for what we believe in. There are no dukes or barons here, thank God.

Haym Salomon set out for America. He arrived in New York in the spring of 1775. Shots had been exchanged between British soldiers and Americans at Lexington and Concord just a few weeks before his arrival. A second Continental Congress, meeting at the State House in Philadelphia, had named George Washington of Virginia as general and commander in chief of an American army.

Haym found a job as a distiller, and in his free time he studied the list of grievances of the thirteen colonies issued by the Congress. The Sons of Liberty demonstrated in New York. And he joined the throng that paraded behind Alexander McDougall down Broad Way to the Battery. He even waved a banner and shouted, like any other patriot, "Give me liberty or give me death!"

Haym Salomon soon gained a reputation for industry and honesty, and before long various Sons of Liberty recommended him as a man "warmly attached to America," which enabled him to become a sutler, or supplier of provisions, for the American troops at Lake George. At the same time he became a ships' provisioner.

Now that he was a respected member of the community, Haym felt it was time to join Shearith Israel Synagogue. But he was too late. The temple had boarded its doors just as the British occupied New York. Moreover, all its members, who were firmly on the side of the Colonies, left their houses and businesses to flee to Philadelphia and other towns still in American hands. Even the young New York–born rabbi, Gershom Seixas, headed north for Stratford, Connecticut, taking with him the sacred Torah scrolls. Jewish youths enlisted in the Continental army.

This last thought brought Haym back to the soldier in his own cellar, at this very moment probably full of despair about being rescued. "Courage, lad,"

Haym murmured. "You will be saved!" Then he thought wryly, And Salomon better not be hanged by the British, for with less than ten Jews left in New York, who would say prayers over my body? Haym began to walk faster.

two

The meeting place lay in the shadow of a deserted windmill a few hundred paces off the road. The night was shot through with gold from a pumpkin moon rising out of the trees, and the seesaw songs of crickets and frogs filled the air. Haym stood waiting and listening.

It was not long before he heard a distant rattling. A horse and wagon emerged from a patch of woods and approached the mill. "Salomon, is that you?" demanded John McClay.

"It is. Any trouble?"

"No. The farmer Van Gelder is on our side. He lent us his rig for the night, with no questions asked." McClay scrambled down from the wagon. "Don't look so serious, friend. I doubt if this is your last trip on earth."

"I don't know. The redcoats are expecting us to react to the fire. Patrols are everywhere!"

"I'd drive the wagon to your house myself," McClay said, "but there's a price on this buck-toothed red head of mine."

"The lad's got a musket ball in his shoulder. When we brought him home he groaned so loudly that my Tory neighbor came to the window in his nightcap. How much he saw or if he reported it, I can't say. But this must be the last time we use my house."

"Aye."

"Besides, I'm a father now. I don't want to get my wife and baby involved if I can help it."

"Well, it was a good hiding place while it lasted. But you've done your part, Haym Salomon, and I'd like to make mash of the man who says you haven't."

Haym pulled himself into the wagon and grasped the reins. "I'll be back as quickly as I can."

"And I'll deliver the lad to Dobbs Ferry."

"Agreed."

"And, Mr. Salomon, relax a bit. In the worst of situations I always sing 'My Bonnie Lies over the Ocean.' Like I haven't a care in the world. It throws suspicious people off the track, and at the same time keeps fear from drying your mouth."

Salomon slapped the reins against the horse's hind quarters, nodded to McClay, and headed into town singing:

"My Bonnie lies over the ocean,
My Bonnie lies over the sea,
My Bonnie lies over the ocean,
Oh, bring back my Bonnie to me."

Salomon kept his voice soft and rolled his r's like a Scotsman. The Scottish burr—another new language. I wager I could be mistaken for a Scot instead of a Jew, he thought, if I tried hard enough. "B-r-r-ring back, b-r-r-ring back, oh, b-r-r-ring back my Bonnie to me."

My bonnie wife, Rachel—am I too old for her? Salomon wondered. A man thirty-eight years of age is certainly not a youth. And a girl of sixteen, Rachel's age, is not quite a woman. They had been married a year and had a two-week-old baby boy, Ezekiel.

Rachel is mature for her years, Salomon reasoned, and I have the energy of a much younger man. Besides, Rachel grew up in luxury and needs a man who knows how to earn a shilling.

Salomon grinned at the memory of Rachel's glee when she first entered the fine house he bought for her. Like a princess she ordered the placement of the gifts from her family. The Chippendale furniture here, the silver tea service and the two sets of china there, the goosedown comforters on their canopied bed. He had even provided his wife with a servant. All he asked in return was one thing—that she be as sympathetic as he was to the Sons of Liberty and the American Revolution.

In the beginning Salomon tried to keep his wife from knowing that he was helping prisoners escape by hiding them in the cellar. But she was too perceptive.

The grunts, the footfalls, the creaking boards in the middle of the night soon made it obvious that men of the Continental army and Hessian deserters were being smuggled in and out.

Without a word to her husband, Rachel ordered extra food to be left on the kitchen table before she went to sleep. She also began to exchange pleasantries with the redcoats when they came to check the premises, to distract them from their purpose with her wit, charm, and dark beauty.

What a splendid young woman! But why shouldn't she be? It was in her blood. Her father, Moses B. Franks, had distinguished himself in service to the Crown of Hannover, Germany, and then the Crown of England. Her Uncle Jacob and cousin David won appointments as Britain's agents for the northern colonies. Her nineteen-year-old brother at this very moment was serving as a lieutenant colonel in George Washington's army. Yes, Rachel was the ideal wife.

A house with a candle or two still burning loomed in the darkness. He would be home soon. The smell of the tanneries traveled the night air, and the stench turned his stomach. Which part of town were the redcoats patrolling with their dogs right now? And where would he be this time tomorrow? He must not think of capture. He recalled how the old Jews of Poland danced in the face of death. He could not dance in the wagon. But he could sing. He would sing all the way home.

> *"B-r-r-ring back, b-r-r-ring back,*
> *Oh, b-r-r-ring back my Bonnie to me."*

three

A light flickered in an upstairs window of the Salomon house. Rachel must be nursing the baby, Haym thought. He reined in the horse, tied it to the hitching post, and let himself into the narrow entrance hallway. His office on the right was dark. But on the left a candle on the mahogany dining-room table revealed a bottle of wine and one of rum, and the chairs were in disarray, as though his wife had been entertaining while he'd been gone.

"Rachel," he called up the stairs. A slip of a girl with dark ringlets and pale skin appeared. "Thank God you're back," she cried. "A British patrol searched the house tonight!"

"What did you do?"

"Everything to distract them—gave them drinks, played the spinet. I was so frightened."

"My poor girl."

"They got drunk and forgot to look in the cellar."

"Lucky the boy didn't groan."

"He did. But the baby began to cry just at that moment and drowned out all else. I asked them to leave so I could nurse my infant. And they went. But they do suspect us." Rachel's eyes grew big. "Haym, I have a feeling of foreboding. Please don't—"

"We must get the soldier out right away. The wagon is outside."

"I spilled the salt and a black cat crossed my path today: bad signs!"

"This will be the last time."

Rachel began to cry. "The patrol has dogs. They'll be waiting for you. If they catch you, it will be the end not only for you but also little Ezekiel and me. We'll be all alone. My parents and all our friends have already left town."

Salomon kissed Rachel's hands. "Have faith in me," he said. Then, taking the candle, he descended the cellar stairs. He wound past the first level, where the bake oven and laundry tubs were, and hurried to the second cellar, which was used to store fruits, vegetables, and wines. The soldier lay there with his right hand pressing tightly against his left shoulder. Rachel had bound his wound with clean rags. Still, he reeked.

"We're going now, laddie," Salomon said to the soldier. "Do you hear me?"

The soldier nodded.

"But you must be very quiet. Can you stand?"

Salomon put a hand under the youth's good shoulder and raised him. "Lean on me. Just put one foot after another up the stairs. Then we'll get into a wagon."

They made their way past the pickling vats and up the steps. Heaving and staggering, Haym got the soldier into the wagon, where he lay face up to the stars, biting his lip. Salomon caught sight of a figure in a window next door. His heart sank. His Tory neighbor had seen everything. Now he must race! He unhitched the horse and jumped into the wagon. At the sting of leather on its haunches, the horse jerked forward. Salomon turned to look at Rachel in the moonlight, perhaps for the last time. She had stopped crying.

Luckily not one street lamp on Broad Way pricked the shadows. Nor could a living creature be seen except for a sow and piglets at the Wall Street intersection and a pack of dogs nosing in a garbage pile near Beekman Street. The barracks came into view. Keep calm, he told himself. No patrol. Not even a sentry. Too good to be true.

He touched the whip to the horse and the big bay broke into a gallop. Ears back, saliva flying, the horse pounded toward the windmill. Just as it came into sight the clatter of a British troop rose behind Salomon. No mistaking that sound. He didn't turn to look. With a "Yah, yah," he urged the horse to race even faster. McClay, he thought, be ready. Be ready!

Haym careened off the road toward the mill. The

wagon lurched around rocks and over ruts, almost bouncing the passenger over the side. "Sorry, boy," Salomon said to the soldier, "but it's the only way to get you through."

McClay jumped out of the shadows and stood poised to jump aboard. Salomon pulled on the reins with all his might. The wagon slowed. McClay swung up before the horse came to a stop.

"Stay on," he shouted to Salomon, "or they'll catch you!"

"They'll catch us *all* if I stay on. They've got to be decoyed. You slip into the woods. It's dark. You know it well. When they stop to arrest me you'll gain a little time." And he jumped down from the wagon.

"Yah!" bellowed McClay to the horse as he cracked the whip over its lathered back. "Good luck, Salomon!" And the wagon streaked for the trees.

The British troop was just turning off the road. Salomon ran out into the moonlight with his hands raised, waving a white handkerchief. His captor, Warden Cunningham, had a reputation for cruelty— they called him "Bloody Bill." Haym knew he was in for it.

four

Warden William Cunningham stood over Haym Salomon like a robin over a worm. "What have we here," he sneered, "but the Jewish revolutionary! They tell me this is the second time you've been arrested. The first time was for sheltering spies and smuggling a message from George Washington himself telling the 'Liberty Boys' to set fire to ships and destroy warehouses. Yes, I've heard all about you and your Sons of Liberty friends!"

Cunningham hated the Sons of Liberty. From Philadelphia they'd passed the word about his brutality there the previous winter of 1777, when British General Howe occupied the city. Witnesses reported that Warden Cunningham had killed with a vicious blow an American prisoner of war who didn't obey his orders and move quickly enough. He was also reported for selling the prisoners' allotment of firewood and their provisions so he could line his own pocket. When General Washington sent a complaint to Lord Howe from his camp at Valley Forge, the British general transferred Cunningham to New York.

For revenge, the Sons of Liberty abducted William Cunningham shortly after his arrival in New York. They forced him to kneel and kiss the Liberty Pole in front of a crowd of jeering patriots. Haym knew this humiliation was still fresh in the warden's mind.

Cunningham scowled. "You were lucky last time you were in jail, Salomon. Because you could speak German, you were used as an interpreter. And no sooner did you gather those German-speaking Hessians around you than you convinced them all to desert! But General Heister set you free to save the British the cost of your food and cot. You are such a fool. Since you were lucky enough to escape one time, why test your luck again?"

Haym thought it best not to reply.

"Last time we imprisoned you in the Sugar House, but this time I'm locking you in 'Congress Hall,'" Cunningham said sourly, "with the other 'outstanding guests.' You'll stay there until you are sentenced to death by the court-martial."

In the darkness and filth of the officers' part of Provost Prison, which the warden had nicknamed "Congress Hall" because it held more or less distinguished American prisoners, Salomon found himself surrounded by leaning, sprawling, spitting, mumbling, moaning, raving men. All begged him for news. Had any new battles been won? Had France sent troops? Was he going to hang, and if so, could they trade their tattered clothes for his since he would never need a pair of breeches again?

Salomon considered the possibilities for escape. He had found a way out of more difficult places. Surely he could make a plan and try it before the foul air and food took his strength and dulled his brain, and before the sickness he had contracted during his last stay in prison attacked him. How? How to get on the other side of the bars?

Within days his old illness flared up. Fits of coughing doubled him up with pain. He lay in a feverish bundle on the floor of the cell with no water to drink, no space to stretch out. He felt relieved when he was dragged from the cell for his court-martial, even though Sir Henry Clinton would surely sentence him to death.

Four British officers heard the charges against Haym Salomon and found the accused guilty of treasonable and seditious acts against the armies of His Majesty King George III. He would hang by the neck until dead on the gallows behind the jail. The execution was scheduled for the following morning.

Was this possible? Was it really happening to him? He'd witnessed the execution of a schoolteacher, Nathan Hale—an ugly end. Frantically, Salomon cried out, "Has Your Excellency no need for an interpreter? I speak German, French, Dutch—"

"Not this time, Jew." The officers turned their backs.

Haym was hustled into the solitary death cell. He sank down onto the bench, his head in his hands. Was there no hope?

In the corridor two Hessians argued in German. "Were you asked if you wanted to come to America?" one said. "What is this British cause to us?"

Salomon smiled bitterly. All his knowledge of languages, his study of Torah, of Jewish ethics and law—was it all to be wasted? He thought back to Lissa, Poland. His father beckoned to him out of the past. The old man held a book in one hand and a honey pot in the other. "Come, Haym," he said, "it is time for you to learn to read."

And Salomon remembered how he had sat on his father's lap as the bearded man opened the great volume.

"We are Jews," his father said, "the people of the Book. When you can read, this Book will be yours. My father gave it to me long ago."

Haym looked at the black designs that made words on the page. Each word was a work of art—dots, curls, loops, dashes, beautiful Hebrew words, like ocean waves running to shore. It would be exciting to learn what the words said.

His father trailed some honey under the first sentence. "As you recognize the words you may lick the honey. In this way, you may come to understand that learning is sweet. Now point to the words and say after me, 'In the beginning . . .'"

"In the beginning—"

"God created the heaven and the earth."

"God created the heaven and the earth."

He enjoyed many winter hours on his father's lap in the big chair. It was warm by the stove in their cottage. The windows, frosted over, were jeweled by rays of afternoon sun. The wind moaned in the cracks of the door, but the sound didn't frighten Haym. He was never afraid with his father there. His father was so strong. He had a straight back, powerful arms, a deep resonant voice. And stronger than his strength was his kindness.

Now he heard the click of heels on wet stone in the corridor. A ruddy face appeared at the cell door. One of the Hessian guards.

"Can you speak my language, prisoner?"

"Yes."

The Hessian unlocked the door and entered. He lowered his voice. "I hear your Washington is offering one hundred acres of good land to any Hessian who deserts the British and joins him. Is it true?"

"It is true." Hope stirred in Haym. "You Hessians are well trained. You fight well. Washington needs you."

"One hundred acres! That's more than a baron would own in my country."

"Yes, and the general promises one hundred more as soon as you can plow them."

"Impossible. You are lying!"

"I am to meet my Maker tomorrow. I would not lie."

The guard sat down on the bench, considering.

"If someone wanted to get to General Washington, how would he find him?"

"He would have to leave the British and contact certain agents."

"The British execute Hessians who try to desert."

"If they can capture them."

The guard rose to peer into the corridor, then returned to the bench. In an excited whisper he said, "I've always longed to own land. The British and I mean nothing to each other. I'm here only because a wretched grand duke sold me along with twenty thousand other German soldiers, like a cannon or a musket, to King George. The grand duke received a generous bonus to put in his pocket for delivering me, I assure you. They pay me a few cents a day. But this is not my cause. A soldier needs a cause."

"The American cause is worth fighting for. Liberty from unjust rulers like your grand duke. Liberty for you and for me!"

The Hessian heard a sound in the corridor. Signaling that he would be back, he hurried out and locked the door behind him. A little later he thrust a quill pen, paper, and ink at Salomon. "Write a note to one of your agents to get me to General Washington. And tell me where to find that agent."

"Here is an address. When the person at this address sees my signature he will see that you are taken safely to the general. It will take a few days. Now I must ask you a favor in return for this signature."

"Yes?"

"I ask you to leave my cell door unlocked."

"Write the note quickly," said the guard.

Salomon looked into the cold gray eyes of the

soldier. They revealed nothing. Would the Hessian free him once he was given the pass? He wrote the message, signed it, and handed it to the Hessian.

"Remain on your bench," the guard ordered as he walked into the corridor and locked the door behind him. Salomon's heart sank. He had gambled and lost. Mercenaries had no honor. A condemned Jew meant nothing to them. Why give Haym an opportunity to flee? But in a minute the Hessian came back and peered through the bars of the cell.

"Prisoner," he whispered, "I'm unlocking the door. I've decided that if my new general is to win the war and give me land, he not only needs me, he needs you, too."

A short while later Haym Salomon was breathing the fresh air outside the prison. He realized it would be foolish to go back to his own house and dangerous for his family. He must slip out of New York and go to the Dobbs Ferry encampment. To do this he must ask Van Gelder or some other farmer sympathetic to the cause to hide him till nightfall, when he would be able to walk in the creeks so as to confuse the hounds of the British.

Haym fell in with a procession of farm carts headed home from the New York produce market. He pictured his prison record: "August 11, 1778, escaped by bribing jailer. Disappeared from New York City, leaving behind six thousand pounds sterling (to be confiscated), wife, and two-week-old boy."

On the outskirts of town he began to run. Struggling through unfamiliar terrain by night and hiding by day, he finally reached Dobbs Ferry. There, his feet blistered, muscles aching, shirt tattered, hair full of burrs, face grimy, he sank against the barricade, unable to go one step farther.

"Who goes there?" a guard in the uniform of the Continental army challenged.

"Haym Salomon, escaped prisoner from the Provost." He could scarcely make himself heard.

"Let me help you," said the voice.

five

When Salomon had recovered from his ordeal he explored the camp with a young lieutenant. The Continental northern force was a sorry sight. No one owned a complete uniform, a new musket, or an unbent bayonet, it seemed. Lean men in buckskin shirts, coonskin caps, and shoes tied together with rope stood around idly outside their patched tents. Salomon had heard of the poverty of some members of the

American force but to actually see these conditions shook him up badly.

He turned to his guide. "Along the road I saw a huge pile of shoes, stockings, jackets, and caps that looked as if they'd been left there for the army's use a long time ago. Haven't you some way to get the supplies?"

"No. The teamsters left those things beyond our reach. They won't work without pay and they say our paper money's no good."

Salomon shook his head in disbelief. "This is an area of plentiful harvest. Why don't the farmers bring you their produce to feed the men?"

"Their sympathies are with us, but they feel they have to feed their families first. The British pay in gold, you know. Our worthless paper can't compete with gold."

How then could these fighting men still be in good spirits, Haym wondered. You would think such hardships would destroy an army. Yet toughened veterans all around him seemed to take pride in the fact that they were not splendid to look at. They had learned it takes more than a red jacket to make a fighting man.

"The new recruits are itching for a big battle," the lieutenant confided.

"And the older men? The veterans?"

"Well, they worry about their families."

The soldiers in the Continental army were not getting their pay to send home to wives, children, and mothers. Congress had not yet found a means of financing the war. The delegates in the Pennsylvania State House could scarcely cover their own bill for firewood. No wonder the soldiers found it necessary to go home for spring planting and not return until after harvest. And could anyone blame those men who took to the towns long enough to earn a little money for their families before they rejoined their group? The escort admitted to Haym that many never came back.

"Who's in command of the forces in this area now?" Salomon asked.

"All troops encamped between Dobbs Ferry and White Plains are under General Alexander McDougall."

McDougall! Then he had given up the leadership of the Sons of Liberty and moved into the field.

Alexander McDougall rose to shake Salomon's hand. His head almost touching the ceiling of the hut that served as headquarters, he was the very picture of a fighting officer. Haym could not help thinking about John Adams's description of him: "He's a very sensible man and an open one. He has none of the mean cunning which disgraces so many of my countrymen."

McDougall smiled delightedly. "Mr. Haym Salomon! So you've cheated the enemy again!"

"You look so splendid, general, I'm overwhelmed."

"I'm very glad you made it." The general kept pumping Salomon's hand, elated by the thought that this skinny, unimposing man had slipped out of the tightest-security prison, out of the very jaws of the British lion—not once but twice. He waved Salomon to a seat.

"Is the Provost still as hellish as it was when I was there?"

"Worse. They still haven't cleaned it."

"Do those poor jam-packed prisoners form a solid wedge when they try to sleep?"

"Some are forced to stand. They're the lucky ones."

"We used to have to lie together in a solid wedge until someone's bones ached and he'd call out, 'Right to left turn!' And the whole compact mass would turn. Then maybe an hour later, 'Left to right turn!' And the whole mass would turn again." McDougall packed tobacco into his clay pipe, lit it, and puffed. "I can laugh about it now."

His expression turned serious. "Actually, the British did me a favor by putting me in prison in 1770. I was fighting a war that hadn't even begun. This made people pay attention to me and the cause. I came out famous. Sympathizers flocked to dine and breakfast with me. Gave me gifts of food and wine. I even had to publish a card showing the times when I would receive the public. You might say prison was the making of me."

Haym started to cough. "It only made me sick."

"You've served well, Salomon. I wouldn't have given a dollar for your chances of getting away from Cunningham."

"I hope this isn't the end of my service."

"I could look into getting a commission for you. There's talk of forming a Jewish Legion of four hundred men under Major Benjamin Nones."

Salomon's eyes brightened. Yes, shouldering arms—that was the proper way to fight a war. But he was almost forty years old now and had a chronic illness. He also had a wife and child. Sadly, he realized his time to be a soldier had passed. But there must be something he was equipped to do. A plan formed in Haym's mind.

"You know, general, until today I thought all that was needed to make a successful fight against tyranny were noble words and outraged young men. But after touring the post it struck me that if the Revolution is lost it will be for lack of money to feed and clothe the soldiers, to supply them with guns and ammunition, and to pay them so that their families aren't in want while they serve."

"I wish all the Congress could see the same appalling sight," commented the general. "The delegates are too timid to ask for money from each of the Colonies. That would be too much like taxation. And taxation is why we're fighting, isn't it? 'By what authority could we make such demands?' they ask each other. And so they devote precious weeks, even months, to setting down on paper the aims of the Revolution and giving the army 'legal authority.' Lawyers you know—talk, talk, talk. Every time they postpone action it's a victory for the enemy. Time is on the side of those powerful British."

"Surely some of the great minds in Philadelphia must realize that without a Treasury there can be no new nation. Without money the Revolution will fail."

McDougall smiled sadly. "The congressmen themselves have been warned they might have to serve without pay. With the exception of a few wealthy Philadelphians and Virginia plantation owners, it's bound to mean hardship for them too."

"Then this would be the ideal time for a hard-headed businessman who knows how to earn and manipulate money for the benefit of the new government to step forward," replied Haym.

"But most men with such talent are Tories—conservative, unsympathetic. They're sitting back and waiting for our 'childish' skirmishes to be over and for the British to resume total control. Bankers seldom back hopeless causes, no matter how noble. They're not good investments. And history books rarely mention the names of financiers."

"Surely there must be someone . . ."

"There's one man Congress hopes will take on the job," said McDougall. "His name is Robert Morris."

"Of Willing and Morris." Haym nodded. "The firm is well known even in New York."

"Morris wouldn't vote for the Declaration of Independence," McDougall said, "although he *did* sign it later. He's not the sort of man I like. The day I met him he looked down his nose at me because I was once a milkman. So I looked down my nose at him because his father was a nailmaker in the slums of Liverpool and his grandfather was a sailor. I beat him out too."

"You did? How?"

"My nose is longer to look down."

They both laughed. Then Salomon said seriously, "General, may I have a pass? I'm going to Philadelphia."

"To Philadelphia!"

"Yes. I don't dare go back to New York."

"But you'd have to skirt the British lines and travel all the way through New Jersey to get to Philadelphia. And I can't spare a horse for you. Anyway, what do you intend to do there when you arrive. You don't know anyone—"

"There are Jews in the 'City of Brotherly Love.' "

"If you wait a day or two I can get you a mount."

"No, I can't wait one day, one hour! I'll walk."

"Don't do that, Haym. You're not well."

"All the more reason for haste. I'm going to fight the war more actively than ever in my own way."

McDougall shook his head.

"I am not your responsibility. Don't worry about me. I've always been able to take care of myself and a few others, too," Salomon reassured him.

McDougall watched him as he limped out the door. He shook his head in silent admiration, as Haym Salomon straightened his shoulders and struck out for the heart of the American colonies, one hundred miles away.

six

P

hiladelphia in 1776 was the second largest city in the whole British Empire. With a population of more than thirty thousand people, it stood out as a miniature London in a land of some three million people, most of them farmers. By 1778 the City of Brotherly Love had become the most industrious and prosperous city in the thirteen colonies, as well as the political capital and cultural center.

A year before Haym Salomon arrived in Philadelphia, British troops had defeated George Washington's men at Germantown, eight miles outside the city, and the Americans had retreated to Valley Forge. Sir William Howe and his army settled into snug Philadelphia homes for the cold winter months of 1777–78. There were plenty of Tories in the Quaker City to make the redcoats welcome. Some of them sincerely loved England, which they considered to be their mother country, and thought it traitorous to fight against King George. Others, who had become rich landowners under the British, opposed the war as a threat to their fortunes. Nor did the Friends (or Quakers as they were often called), whose forebears had settled Philadelphia one hundred years earlier, pose a problem to the occupying force. Most Friends held strictly to their religious principle of peace and refused to take up arms for any reason at all.

In their splendid uniforms and powdered wigs, the British officers wooed Philadelphia ladies at balls, dinners, and masquerade parties. They flaunted their wealth, power, and disdain for the ragged American beggars freezing at Valley Forge in the company of their beloved General Washington. Why leave? Why exchange the comfort and luxury of Philadelphia for a sure but chilly victory, they reasoned, when the enemy could be defeated by starvation and exposure?

General Howe made a serious mistake. For during the winter, while he and his fellow officers danced, a Prussian baron named von Steuben, who had been attracted to the cause of liberty, volunteered his services to the Continental army. Day after day von Steuben drilled the men at Valley Forge in the use of the bayonet and cannon. Hundreds of new recruits made their way to Valley Forge to be molded into crack soldiers by the Prussian.

With the coming of spring, Howe had had second thoughts about attacking Valley Forge. Since his men were soft after a winter of pleasure, such a move might prove foolish. Naturally, he did not want to risk a loss. So he decided instead to join his compatriots in New York to form an overwhelming force that would crush the Americans.

Upon hearing that Howe intended to leave Philadelphia, the Tories, along with Howe's own officers, put on a great pageant in the general's honor. It was called a *meschianza* (an Italian word meaning medley or mixture), and the man who arranged it all was a handsome and brilliant young officer, Major John André.

A spectacle such as the *meschianza* had never been seen in the Colonies. British officers and beautiful ladies of the city sailed down the Delaware River in decorated boats, while bands played and cannons on shore saluted their progress. They landed at an estate called Walnut Grove.

In a mock medieval tournament seven Knights of the Blended Rose tilted with seven Knights of the Burning Mountain on the bank of the river. Men in colorful costumes mounted on horses demonstrated the ancient skill of jousting, while the ladies sitting nearby served as inspiration.

When the exhibition was over the guests gathered for a ball in a mansion on the riverbank. Blue flowers, priceless paintings, and a galaxy of mirrors created an extravagantly beautiful setting. Fireworks lit the sky at midnight, and a supper was served to four hundred persons in a long hall. Slaves in brilliant turbans and silver bracelets and collars padded to and fro, serving the guests. Hundreds of candles suspended from the ceiling and mounted on the walls lit the scene as the ladies and their escorts danced through the night. Never did they give a thought to the wretches at Valley Forge.

The cocky British Army paraded out of Philadelphia on June 18, 1778, in time to drumbeats. Tory families trailed behind. Their cockiness soon vanished, for they marched right into the tough beggar army von Steuben had drilled at Valley Forge, who were now waiting to surprise them at Monmouth, New Jersey. The Americans dealt the British a telling defeat.

Congress returned to the State House in Philadelphia in the summer of 1778. Never again would the capital city fall into the hands of the enemy.

The British had left Philadelphia a shambles. The pebblestone streets of the neat checkerboard town were cluttered with rubbish. British horses had been stabled in schools and churches, decorative fences had been torn down and used as firewood, gardens had been trampled. The homes of people favoring independence had been vandalized and burned. Worst of all, the interior of the State House was in terrible condition after being used as a prison.

But none of these scars could be seen from the Delaware River in September of '78, when the keelboat carrying Haym Salomon threaded its way through sloops, schooners, square-riggers, and brigs riding at anchor in the bay. When the boat touched shore at Dock Creek, Haym scrambled onto the pier.

What he saw there made his head spin: casks of gunpowder, crates of tobacco, wheat, corn, hemp, flax, rolls of fabrics, bales of cotton, lumber, salted fish, and beef in barrels piled three high.

There's a cargo from Jamaica that will bring a pretty penny, Salomon thought. And look at all that merchandise! This must be spoils captured in the North Sea by a privateer. (Lacking a navy, the Congress had commissioned private owners of boats to arm their vessels and pirate British shipping. These were called privateers.) He noticed men inspecting and recording the goods, and in the background he heard the familiar babble of buying and selling by brokers. Time and again angry voices demanded "hard money," not the paper dollars issued by the Congress. So, even the people who lived in the shadow of the Liberty Bell had no faith in the outcome of the American Revolution!

Much as he wanted to explore every wharf that fingered into the Delaware north as far as he could see, Haym put that aside for another time. A pair of sailors swinging into the Blue Anchor Inn on Dock Street reminded him that he was very hungry and tired. But he hadn't a penny to spend. He had heard in New York of the Gratz brothers, who had found success in Philadelphia. He must seek them and ask for help. Looking as wretched as he did after his long flight from Dobbs Ferry, Haym hesitated to ask directions of anyone. But finally he approached a black-clad man counting barrels.

"Sir," he began, "can you tell me where the Gratz brothers live?"

The man eyed him suspiciously. "I trust you do not want to make trouble for them. They're good Hebrews, prayerful men."

"No, I'm a Jew myself, recently escaped from the British prison in New York."

The man eyed him from head to toe.

"I look this way because I walked most of the way from Dobbs Ferry. See, I have a pass from General McDougall."

The man read the pass.

"I have no knowledge of your city and no money with me. If you direct me to my brethren they'll help me, I know. A Jew does not refuse a Jew. All Israel is responsible for one another."

"Neither would a Quaker turn you away." The man returned the pass. "I don't know this fighting McDougall. But I do know the peaceful Hebrew named Barnard Gratz. I've done business with him and his brother Michael for twenty years. B. and M. Gratz is located at 107 Race Street."

Salomon followed the Quaker's directions, admiring Philadelphia as he went. Unlike Europe's age-old capitals, which had begun as castle-fortresses with webs of dark alleys spun around them or America's colonial cities that just grew randomly, Philadelphia had been planned by William Penn as the commercial center, the capital of the vast province of Pennsylvania. And before any settlers arrived, Penn had ordered it laid out in the most sensible way, in a grid of straight streets from the Delaware River to the Schuylkill River. Numbered streets ran north and south, those with names ran east and west. There were parks and gardens and tree-lined avenues with brick sidewalks.

Haym found the Gratz place of business. "But Mr. Gratz is at worship," he was told.

"Where?"

"At Mr. Joseph Cauffman's house in Cherry Alley between Third and Fourth Streets." Philadelphia had no synagogue as yet.

Salomon found the Cauffman residence. Men were assembling for evening devotions in a large room fitted for Hebrew services. A card on the door read CONGREGATION MIKVEH ISRAEL. He kissed the mezuzah on the doorpost and entered.

The sight of this group of Jews in prayer shawls, swaying and chanting words that harked back to his boyhood, warmed Haym Salomon. Here he was no stranger, no beggar. Here he would find the most charitable hearts. He slipped into the group and joined in the ancient Hebrew prayers.

seven

When the service ended the men welcomed Salomon and heard his story. Sympathetic to his cause, they first assured him that Rachel and the baby would be smuggled out of New York and brought to Philadelphia as soon as possible. Two men who were the leaders of the Jewish business community volunteered to advance him enough money to get started in business again, on condition that he appeal to the Continental Congress for the $30,000 he lost while working for the Revolution.

"You won't get paid, that we know," the distinguished Isaac Moses said. "But where a contribution has been made for the American cause, it's better for the Jewish community at this time to have it be on record."

Salomon agreed to write an appeal. When the others left, Barnard Gratz conducted Salomon to the Gratz home.

For the first time in a month Haym Salomon sat in a comfortable wing-backed chair in a gracious house. The two men talked and sipped wine.

"Isaac Moses is the leader of our congregation. He replaced a man who is now serving under George Washington."

"Philadelphia seems a comfortable place for Jews," Haym said.

"For all sorts of minority groups. Pennsylvania was conceived as a haven for persecuted people. If a man is honest and hardworking it's the City of Brotherly Love for him, no matter what his religion. If through ingenuity and sweat he makes a lot of money in business, Philadelphia respects him.

"The Jewish community is growing because of the war. I can remember when we had less than fifty families here. Now we number hundreds. It wouldn't surprise me if the Jews who came here after the British left in the spring settle here for good. God willing that we win independence, of course."

"Are most of you merchants in Philadelphia?"

"A good number—like my younger brother Michael and myself. For about twenty years we've supplied the government with Indian goods. With God's help we've been quite successful. Even in New York you must have heard of our oldest and most prestigious Jewish firm, Levy and Franks. Their ship, the *Myrtilla,* has brought all sorts of luxuries from London, including the very bell in the State House that rang out the news that the Congress had passed the Declaration of Independence!"

"What have the merchants done to show where they stand on the Revolution?"

"They all signed agreements not to import British goods until the Stamp Act was repealed. We've had very few Tories in our midst, and our people have contributed their money generously to the cause. Isaac Moses for example, has already given $15,000 to the Treasury and Hayman Levy—"

A servant announced dinner. Haym enjoyed the kosher food and wine of the Gratz table. But soon after dessert he began to nod. Gratz insisted that his guest retire to a third-floor bedroom, where clean clothes were laid out for the next morning.

Haym settled down with a sigh into the comfortable big bed, the first he'd slept in for many weeks. He thanked God for rescuing him from prison in New York and for delivering him to friends. He prayed that Rachel and Ezekiel would soon be with him.

eight

Salomon rested only briefly in Gratz's home. Following the advice of his new friends, he worked on a petition to the Continental Congress. In spite of his exhaustion, he felt he must get to work to actively help the Revolutionary cause. On the twenty-fifth of August he finished his "memorial."

To the Honorable, the Continental Congress

The Memorial of Haym Salomon, late of the city of New York, merchant, humbly showeth

That your memorialist was some time before the entry of the British troops at the City of New York and soon after taken up as a spy and by General Robertson committed to the Provost. That by the interposition of Lieutenant General Heister (who wanted him on account of his knowledge of French, Polish, Russian, Italian, etc. languages) he was given over to the Hessian commander who appointed him... as purveyor chiefly for the officers. That being at New York he has been of great service to the French and American prisoners and has assisted them with money and helped them to make their escape. That this and his close connection with such of the Hessian officers as were inclined to resign... has rendered him so obnoxious to the British headquarters that he was... rearrested ...on Tuesday the 11th inst., he made his happy escape from thence....

At this point in the memorial, Salomon inserted a plea to the Congress for their aid in obtaining the release of a fellow prisoner. Then he went on:

Your memorialist has upon this event most irrecoverably lost all his effects and credits to the amount of five or six thousand pounds sterling and left his distressed wife and child of a month old at New York waiting that they may soon have an opportunity to come out from thence with empty hands.

In these circumstances he most humbly prayeth to grant him any employ in the way of his business whereby he may be enabled to support himself and family — and your memorialist in duty bound, etc., etc.

Haym Salomon
Philadelphia, August 25th, 1778

As expected, the Continental Congress ignored the appeal.

Haym, anxious to get established, explored Philadelphia. These people seem to pray a lot and drink a lot, Haym thought, as he counted twenty-two churches of many denominations and twice as many taverns. The food market on Market Street that stretched from the Delaware River west for three blocks impressed him, for it was the largest he had ever seen.

Barnard Gratz showed him various points of interest in the city and pointed out the pride of the Quaker City, the State House where the Continental Congress had affirmed that all men have the right to "life, liberty, and the pursuit of happiness." (Later the State House was called Independence Hall to commemorate that ideal.) He saw where the University of Pennsylvania had been started and vowed to himself that someday his son would study there. Last, Gratz showed him the Jewish graveyard at Eighth and Spruce Streets.

Haym bought a copy of each of the four local newspapers to read their editorials and their advertisements. He found a silk handkerchief advertised for $40, a hat for $400. You could buy a pair of leather breeches for $300 and a pair of shoes for $125. Fishhooks could be had for fifty cents each.

Finally he went down to the waterfront to talk to the seamen in their native tongues. Their stories about slipping into ports to trade, in the shadow of the British fleet, interested him. A raid on a British ship in the Mediterranean could yield rich booty for an American privateer. One captain pointed out vessels riding at anchor in the Delaware with cargoes from Madeira, Lisbon, Italy, and the West Indies. Clearly, for his purposes the most important section of Philadelphia would be the waterfront.

One day Salomon saw a well-dressed, portly man climb aboard a ship with two clerks following him. He seemed to command so much respect that Haym asked a seaman if this gentleman could be Robert Morris.

"Aye," the seaman affirmed, "that's just who he be. When the war started Mr. Morris armed all his vessels with cannon and turned them loose on the shipping lanes to capture cargo."

"Like pirating."

The man looked hurt. "Why, sir, Britain is our enemy! The crew aboard a privateer sees it as a navy ship. With a nice difference," he confided. "The crew gets a share of the profits! The enemy get hurt."

"And the owner gets rich."

A great deal of business was transacted in the Front Street coffeehouses. Haym passed many hours there. He listened to the talk of profits and losses, contracts and markets, ships and ship captains and ship owners, francs, pistoles, shillings, pounds, and thalers, and the disorganization and looming bankruptcy of the Revolution.

He noted which men were generous, which mean, which showed good judgment, which were good-natured fools, which false, which honest, and which dependable. He saw that few businessmen, even if they had read through the document, understood the implications of the Declaration of Independence; less than half of them cared desperately whether America won the war. But all worried about their personal profits! They publicly berated the Continental

Congress because it now took $525 in paper Continental dollars to buy one silver dollar. To show their contempt they lined their hats with the paper bills or burned them as fuel in their Franklin stoves. Disgusted, Haym Salomon reaffirmed his vow that any profit he could make, as long as there was a need, would be used largely to aid the Continental Congress and its army.

It became his routine to take a table at the coffeehouse, where he began to buy and sell goods with money his friends had advanced him. At first the established men referred to him as the "haggler Jew," then as the "Jew broker." They insulted him, slighted him, ignored him. But drawing on the wisdom gained in his years of trade in many lands before he came to America, Salomon started to make business transactions that yielded a profit every time. His tormentors sat up and took notice.

Scrupulously honest but shrewd, Salomon had soon earned enough money to repay his friends, rent an office on Front Street, and hire an assistant named McRae. By the time Rachel and the baby were brought down from New York by Samuel Judah and his family, the "Jew broker" had bought the building his office was in and had made part of it into a comfortable home. At the end of a year he had earned three times the $30,000 taken from him by the British in New York.

One day Salomon read a letter from a man named James Thatcher, printed in the newspaper:

Our poor soldiers are reduced to the very edge of famine, their patience is exhausted by complicated sufferings, and their spirit is almost broken.

Salomon sent a letter to General George Washington expressing his eagerness to serve the army by financing some of its deserving officers. A short time later Baron von Steuben sought an interview with him.

Von Steuben began, "Mr. Salomon, it pains me to ask for money but—"

Salomon nodded and held up his hand. "Sir, you do me a favor to visit me. You are giving me an opportunity to do something for our cause. I know you are paid only if and when Congress can manage it—and then in paper money. God help them, for there's nothing else with which to pay you. The paper wage you are supposed to receive monthly is probably worth about three dollars. Am I correct?"

"Yes, and pity the poor privates. When they get it, their pay is worth about twenty cents a month."

"Congress simply cannot discharge its obligations," Salomon said. "The congressmen feel they can't tax the states when taxation is precisely what we all took up arms to oppose. So in my small way I will help with money wherever I can."

Von Steuben raised his eyebrows.

"Perhaps you think this too presumptuous?" queried Haym.

"No, I think it extraordinary."

"How much do you need?"

Von Steuben took a deep breath. "One thousand pounds."

"You shall have it."

The officer flushed with pleasure. "I accept this as a loan which I hope to repay when the crisis is over. Should I be killed before that time, I expect Congress will honor the debt."

General Casimir Pulaski also came to the Salomon office. The two men spoke in Polish of Tadeusz and Kosciusko, Polish officers now serving in the Continental army.

"After the battle of Germantown, Congress authorized me to raise a mixed corps and call it the Pulaski Legion," the officer finally said.

"What an honor, sir!"

"There will be sixty-eight light horse and two hundred foot soldiers as soon as I can get enough money to equip them."

"When might that be?"

"It might be never, unless . . ." Pulaski paused.

"You wish my help," Salomon suggested.

"Yes. You see, it would be a good thing for leaders of many nationalities to be involved in the battle against tyranny. Don't you agree?"

"I do indeed. I can even envision a company named the Salomon Legion." The broker smiled. "I will give you my financial support. Good luck to you."

nine

For a while every venture Salomon attempted turned out well. The way it worked was simple but risky. A ship would be long overdue. The owner, fearing the worst, would try to find someone who would share his risk by purchasing a percentage of the cargo, someone willing to take a chance on the ship's returning to port.

Haym would investigate the ability of the ship's captain and study the weather over the Atlantic Ocean.

If the information seemed to forecast a successful voyage, Salomon frequently gambled. His ships always seemed to limp home.

Before long the broker's successes attracted attention and envy. Grudgingly the coffeehouse crowd admitted that he used no tricks. Salomon could be counted on for wisdom and integrity. Soon young merchants moved to his table, eager to learn his way of turning a profit.

In his dealings Salomon began to see bills of exchange from foreign countries—notes that promised to pay the bearer the amount specified on the bill. Europeans preferred to pay for American merchandise with such notes. They found it safer than sending money across the ocean. In their loans to the Revolutionary government in America, France and Spain also used bills of exchange. These notes had to be sold for cash in Philadelphia. The seller, by putting his name on the note, made himself responsible for payment in case the original issuer refused to pay.

There was money to be made on the buying and selling of bills of exchange. Frequently a man who owned one worth, say, $100 and needed cash right away, would sell that bill for $90, if that was all he was offered for it. The man who purchased it at $90 might later be able to resell the bill of exchange at the original price. Haym Salomon knew how to handle bills of exchange. Probably there was no other man in America who knew as much as he did about international currency. In addition, he had established a reputation for dependability.

The Treasury of the United States now owed $1.5

million. Robert Morris reluctantly accepted the responsibility of controlling all financial matters and trying to find the money to pay for the Revolution.

Like Salomon, Robert Morris had been born abroad. He had sailed from England at the age of thirteen. Having a limited education, he'd gone from job to job until he was employed as clerk in the Philadelphia commercial house of Willing. About this time Morris's father emigrated to the South, where he died within a few years, leaving $7,000 to his son. At the age of twenty-one Robert Morris became head of the firm now called Willing and Morris. And under his guidance it became the leading importing house in America, with many ships on the sea trading with Europe and the West Indies.

Morris, though as angry as any other American in 1775 at the restrictive measures England had taken against the Colonies, nevertheless opposed the radicals in Congress in 1776 who demanded separation from England. He and other conservatives argued that the Colonies were not prepared militarily and economically for a war with the most powerful empire in the world. And to follow John Adams and the other "wise men from the East" into a revolution would be idiocy. He refused to vote for the Declaration of Independence. And it was not until the measure was adopted that he reluctantly joined the others and signed it.

The wealthy Mr. Morris's experience as head of Willing and Morris made him the obvious choice to be a minister of finance under the Articles of Confederation that were adopted by Congress in 1778. He accepted the post only after protesting, "I am no miracle worker, and miracles will be needed to keep this government out of bankruptcy." Sourly he wrote in his diary:

> *This appointment was unsought, unsolicited and dangerous to accept, as it was evidently contrary to my private interests, and if accepted must deprive me of those enjoyments both social and domestic which my time of life required and which my circumstances entitled me to, and as a vigorous execution of the duties must inevitably expose me to the resentment of disappointed and designing men and to the calumny and detraction of the envious and malicious.*

Within a short time all the fiery young congressmen who had called Morris a Tory for not voting for the Declaration of Independence found they were having problems that only money could solve. They turned to the minister of finance for help.

Morris was soon driven to his wits' end in his efforts to give that help. He went through his own fortune. Then he sought the help of acquaintances—because he was bullheaded, opinionated, and abrupt, he had few real friends to call upon. He went as far as to seek aid from wealthy Quakers, against whom he was said to be prejudiced, in order to raise money. But he couldn't bring himself to ask Jews for assistance.

The minister of finance had been told many times that the broker by the name of Haym Salomon was anxious to aid the Revolution. General Washington himself had said that Salomon periodically sent money directly to him and lent money to officers. But Morris believed Jews lent money only at a high rate of interest and wanted no dealings with Salomon or his kind.

By the fall of 1780 the Continental army had received no pay for five months. From his headquarters in Morristown, Washington sent a plea to Robert Morris for funds.

"I'm doing my best," Morris answered. And he pictured in his mind the deep snows and bitter cold soon to come.

Washington wrote, "Rations are so low as to cause two regiments to assemble, beat drums, and strike down a colonel to get some food. I appeal to you!"

Morris replied, "There are no funds at this moment. Hold on!"

A message about dissatisfied troops reached Morris's desk from New England: "Today the Connecticut Line mutinied en masse. Force had to be used in the shape of Pennsylvania troops!"

And from Washington again, "We have at this day not one ounce of meat, fresh or salt, in the magazine and know of no shipments on the way. The situation is desperate. The army is threatening mutiny. Please see Mr. Salomon."

The minister of finance walked to his office window and stared absently out at the fog-cloaked Delaware River. The seasons were changing. How many days before winter would freeze the river and block shipping? He remembered the agony of Valley Forge, the misery of the troops. Conditions had not improved. By now the burden on Washington must be insupportable. If the general could not supply food and basic equipment for his men, how could he keep enough of them to make an army? Who would be able to persuade the soldiers whose terms were expiring to reenlist?

"Ross!" Morris called in the direction of his office doorway. "Ross!"

"Sir."

"Do you know a broker named Salomon?"

"Mr. Haym Salomon? I do, sir. His office is a short way from here."

"Go and fetch him to me."

A while later the aide returned alone.

"Well, where is he?" demanded Morris.

"Mr. Salomon is not at his office or the coffeehouse. They say that today is one of the Jews' holy days and that—"

"Find him and tell him I want to see him."

"But, sir, out of respect to—"

"This is a matter of life and death for the Revolution. Do you understand?"

"Please don't ask me to go into their place of worship. I'm afraid!"

Morris impatiently grabbed a piece of paper. "You don't have to go in. Just take this letter to the door. Ask if Salomon can do something about it and wait outside for an answer."

ten

For Haym Salomon this Yom Kippur, this Day of Atonement, seemed touched with signs and portents. Haym had awakened to find that fog shrouded the streets of town. The dampness made him cough and struggle for breath. He dragged himself out of bed. He would spend the fast day at Mikveh Israel, praying that God might inscribe him in the Book of Life for yet another year.

He arrived at services damp and coughing and

with a crushed feeling in his chest that reminded him of his first imprisonment in New York's roofless Sugar House. Feeling this way, would he be able to settle down to confession and prayer? There was confusion all around him as the sexton tried to find chairs enough to seat the unexpectedly large crowd.

In one corner Haym saw the Gratz brothers introducing an unfamiliar man to Simon Nathan and Jonas Phillips. He must be Isaac Da Costa of Charleston, South Carolina, Haym thought. All six hundred families of Charleston, the largest community of Jews in America, were sympathetic to independence, and had fled to Philadelphia rather than stay in their own occupied city.

Along the east wall he spotted Rabbi Gershom Mendes Seixas, the congregation's leader, newly arrived from Stratford, Connecticut. There, too, was Jacob Rivera, a refugee from Newport, Rhode Island, and his son-in-law, kissing the corners of their prayer shawls before wrapping them around their shoulders. A few young men on leave from the army sat in places of honor. Later they would be called upon to read from the Torah. Haym's gaze rested on one of them, Philip Moses Russell, the surgeon's mate who had been commended by George Washington for his service at Valley Forge. Russell had draped his prayer shawl over his army tricorn hat, in the ancient Jewish tradition, and opened his prayer book.

The service began with a mournful chant. Haym could not concentrate on the words in his prayer book. Instead, he thought about Jews and revolution. Hebrew Scripture preached rebellion against tyrants: the story of the Exodus from Egypt, for example. He had

heard that Benjamin Franklin, who over the years showed more than average respect for the Jews and the Hebrew Bible, had proposed that when the Revolution was won, the seal of the United States should picture the children of Israel crossing the Red Sea. The

inscription would read, REBELLION TO TYRANTS IS OBEDIENCE TO GOD!

In a discussion at Barnard Gratz's house the week before, Jacob Rivera had described living in a Puritan environment. He told them that the laws the Puritans followed, as well as their guides to personal conduct, were all taken from the Hebrew Scriptures. It amazed Salomon to hear that the Puritan founders of New Haven, in Connecticut, had prescribed the teaching of Hebrew in the city's first public school.

Barnard Gratz joined in. "Philadelphia Christians who have had a classical education," he said, "accept Jews because Hebrew was the language of the Bible. You must know," he added, "that when the Pennsylvania Assembly ordered a bell for the State House in 1751, they chose to have inscribed on it a passage from Leviticus: 'Proclaim liberty throughout all the land and to all the inhabitants thereof.' "

But say what you will, Haym thought, even here in the City of Brotherly Love most Christians still scorn us and deny us some civil rights. His thoughts touched on his little son, Ezekiel, and his new daughter, Sarah, called Sallie. Would these innocent children eventually be persecuted just as the European Jews had been? No, Jews were taking part in this struggle for independence. After winning the war, American Jews must make sure the new government's laws were just!

The morning wore on, the congregation recited prayer after prayer. Young and old stood or sat down as the holy ark was opened or shut. The room grew hot and stuffy.

There was a knock at the door. What fool would knock on Yom Kippur, Salomon wondered.

"Come in, come in, get to your prayers. You're late," he heard the sexton say.

A few minutes later the sexton pushed his way to Haym's side. "Haym," he whispered. His face was red and his eyes startled. "There's someone to see you— a gentile at the door."

"To see me on Yom Kippur?"

"I told him it's the Day of Atonement. I told him he ought to be ashamed to disturb a man at his prayers and that it was disgraceful. But he says he must give you a very important message that can't wait."

Ezekiel must be sick—or the baby—or Rachel. Quickly Salomon moved to the back of the room. Heads turned but the chanting continued. He noticed out of the corner of his eye the elderly Mr. Bush being helped to a chair near a window. A soldier rapped his breast for each sin he might have committed as he sang his plea for God's forgiveness.

"Couldn't this have kept till tomorrow?" he demanded of the young man standing at the door.

"Mr. Robert Morris made me come, sir. It's urgent. I have a letter for you. I'm to wait for an answer."

"Robert Morris!"

Hastily he broke the seal and found two bills of exchange and a note.

My Dear Mr. Salomon:

The terrible emergency of the moment necessitates my turning to you at this hour.

The office of finance has been unable to procure sufficient funds to cover the enclosed notes, which must be discounted immediately.

I have exhausted even my personal sources of aid.

Since all else has failed, I must beg of you to act immediately with whatever resources you have to satisfy our distress.

72

"This day of all days!" Salomon muttered bitterly. "When Jews close their shops, empty their pockets of every penny, put all thoughts of money from their minds. He chooses this holy day!"

Then he reread the note, focusing his attention on the last sentence: "Since all else has failed, I must beg of you. . . ."

"Wait here," he ordered the messenger.

Reentering the house, Haym strode to the bima and prodded Rabbi Seixas. "I must address the congregation, rabbi. "I have here a message from Robert Morris—a matter of extreme urgency."

"Financial communications on Yom Kippur? It is forbidden!"

"Rabbi, the Continental Congress and the army are desperate. I demand to speak, may God forgive me!"

Rabbi Seixas stepped aside and Salomon read Morris's note aloud. Shouts of outrage filled the room.

"How dare you?"

"You are defiling our ears!"

"Have you lost your mind?"

"What is the meaning of this?"

Patiently Salomon explained. "We are losing as many soldiers from starvation and cold as we are from British bayonets. There's a threat of mutiny in General Washington's camp. Do we want this country with its promise of freedom to be truly our country? We have longed for such a place to live more than any other people. Let us pledge our dollars immediately to cover these notes to help the Revolution succeed. Mr. Morris must have $20,000!"

A hush fell on the worshipers.

"We're known for aiding the suffering both inside and outside our own circle. But now we must show that above all we are true patriots. Sexton, ask Mr. Morris's aide to come in and record the amount of our pledges. I'll pledge $3,000."

"And I'll pledge $3,000 too," exclaimed Isaac Moses.

Samuel Lyon rose from his chair and cried out, "I pledge $1,000, and may God forgive me!"

Jonas Phillips spoke for $250 dollars and Hayman Levy for $500. In fifteen minutes pledges for the $20,000 had been raised.

"Now will you leave us in peace, Salomon," a voice called from the congregation. "We've lost communion with the Lord."

They pulled their prayer shawls up and fell to praying for forgiveness.

Salomon followed Morris's aide to the door. "Tell me, young man, did you ever see such evidence of patriotism before?"

"No, sir, and I know I never shall again."

"After sundown tonight Mr. Morris shall have his money."

News of Salomon's devotion to the Revolution spread through Philadelphia. When General Benedict Arnold, in dire need, had gone to the French minister for a loan he had been referred to Salomon.

"You are looking at a bitter man," Arnold told the broker. "You've heard about my trouble. Everyone in Philadelphia must know that I've been humiliated by the Executive Council of this city, accused of overstepping my authority as commander of Philadelphia.

"And what is worse, they've accused me of Tory leanings. I suppose that must be because I married a Loyalist's daughter!

"Would you believe it, Mr. Salomon, I am in such debt that I am considering giving up soldiering? What should I do? The Pennsylvania Legislature has persecuted me, and the country too is ungrateful."

"I've heard you were courageous in all your battles and that you were seriously wounded."

"Wounded! I've been crippled. I can't walk and I can't ride a horse. I'm not even fit to offer military advice. They'll want me in the future, I'm sure. But if they can't use me now, and they can't pay me now, how am I to get along from day to day? What is to become of me—a crippled veteran betrayed by politicians! I'm resentful all right. Can you blame me?"

"It's hard not to be bitter, but the Congress has many difficult problems and no experience. We must have faith in them."

"You will never know how it feels to be shunned by everyone."

"General Arnold, I've been a prisoner of war twice and had my house, business, and all my savings taken by the British in New York. From a penniless condition I have had to struggle back."

Arnold looked incredulous.

"No payments were ever made to me by the Congress," Salomon went on. "But this hasn't made me lose faith in the cause. I'll continue fighting in the way I know best, the only way I'm now able to wage war. You shall have your money."

Benedict Arnold rose and bowed. "I believe I am talking to a true American patriot. It's sad you will receive none of the glory. That seems reserved for Washington's favorites. Nor will you get any of the spoils of war. Those go to the politicians. I suppose you will have to content yourself merely with the thanks of bitter men like myself."

When Arnold left, Salomon opened his ledger. Here he had recorded the names of the many patriots to whom he had given loans. These men hadn't allowed themselves to lose sight of the goals for which they were fighting. They weren't swayed by personal ambition, nor were they embittered by the lack of

support or the still greater obstacles yet to be over-
come.

Among the names listed in his ledger were those
of many of the most famous officers and politicians of
the day.

eleven

L ife in Philadelphia brimmed with excitement for young Rachel Salomon. Philadelphia had long been the reigning cultural and commercial center of the Colonies, and now it accommodated not only the Pennsylvania provincial and Philadelphia governments, but also the Continental Congress, in its State House. Men important to the struggle for independence passed Rachel in the street every day. More than once Haym had pointed out Mr. John Adams of Massachusetts and a tall handsome fellow with red hair named Thomas Jefferson, "a young Virginian of great promise."

Rachel had hoped to see with her own eyes the most famous man in America, Dr. Benjamin Franklin. Her interest in Franklin lay not in his discoveries in electricity but in his writings. As a child, Rachel had learned to read from a copy of Franklin's *Poor Richard's Almanack.* The book now stood on the Salomon shelf next to the Hebrew Bible and prayer book. Unlike other tomes, Poor Richard not only gave Rachel good advice but made her laugh too. The wise and amusing Dr. Franklin, however, had sailed to France in 1776 to bring about an alliance between France and America and stayed on there as envoy.

On sunny days Rachel strolled with little Ezekiel through the market that extended along Market Street from Front to Fourth Street. Or they walked over to the State House, where jugglers, acrobats, or dancing bears occasionally performed in the yard. Sometimes she called on friends for tea. The ladies discussed dressmakers, remedies for illnesses, needlepoint rugs, and the new fashion of pasting printed papers on parlor walls. Comfortable Philadelphia Jews, like most of their fellow citizens, loved diversion. They dined at each other's homes and passed many evenings with music and conversation.

The snug brick Salomon house looked onto the Delaware River. It had a kitchen in the basement and an ice cellar below that. The Salomons kept a cow on the enclosed ground to the rear of their home, and an outhouse or "necessary" stood in a far corner of the property. They owned a horse and a chaise. There were pleasant neighbors on either side and many children for Ezekiel and Sallie to play with. Most important to Rachel, her husband had found a satisfying occupation in Philadelphia and had quickly established a fine reputation.

Rachel knew Jews were working at various occupations in the South and New England. They were shopkeepers, plantation owners, fur traders, merchants, and some traveled the primitive frontier roads as peddlers. But Haym's occupation seemed the most natural path to success for a Jew. With friends or relatives in European ports as agents in the complicated handling of imported and exported cargoes, he had many advantages.

One thing dimmed Rachel's joy in life in Philadelphia, however. Her husband did not share his worries over money with her. His love was tender and protective. He wished, as a father might wish, that he could keep this precious child, Rachel, from worries forever. But gossip reached her ears that a good deal of the hundreds of thousands of dollars Haym had earned since he came to the Quaker City he had insisted on lending to the Congress and its officials. Her best friends warned her that Haym seemed to care more for the War of Independence than he did for the security of his family—that he was sacrificing his health to impress Mr. Robert Morris.

Even Haym's assistant began to resent the unreasonable demands on his employer. One day McRae revealed to Rachel that Congress had asked Haym to advance a whole year's pay to Mr. Jones, Mr. Randolph, and Mr. Madison of the Continental Congress.

"That's going too far," McRae said angrily.

"Did Haym pay them?" Rachel asked.

"Not only did he pay what Congress requested, but when he noticed they had allotted Madison fifty pounds less than the other two, he corrected the situation by giving them all the same amount out of his own pocket."

"But why?"

"Because he said he saw something in this twenty-nine-year-old Madison that he liked. Some special promise, he said."

"Forgive me, friend McRae," Rachel said, "but was that a bad thing to do? It seems to me a simple kindness, an act of encouragement."

"Out of his own pocket? Fifty pounds no one asked him for? It may not have been a bad thing, but it just wasn't necessary."

"My dear, dear man."

"Well you might say, 'dear, dear man,' "McRae grumbled, "but I'd like to hear others being so appreciative. Judge James Wilson would have had to retire from public service for lack of money if it hadn't been for Haym. Did Haym ever receive thanks? No. And let me read you some of the famous names on the latest list of people he supports: John Paul Jones, Marquis Charles Armand Taffin, General Daniel Morgan, Thomas Jefferson, Thaddeus Kosciusko, General Benjamin Lincoln—"

"Enough, enough. I never knew."

"Of course you never knew—that's the way he is," McRae went on. "No one will ever know about Haym Salomon, master of delicacy and kindness. The great speechmakers and brave soldiers—they'll go down in history because of the help your husband gave them. But mark my words, he will wear himself out and die poor and unknown—the dear, dear man."

"Haym," Rachel said one evening, "you're so thin. You're working too hard. Why don't you take a little rest, so you won't get sick."

"Don't worry, Rachel," Salomon said reassuringly. "I'm not an old man yet. I don't need a rest. Time for that in the grave."

Rachel summoned up the courage to ask, "Haym, if you stopped working, would we have enough money to live on? I mean, wouldn't it be better if I knew something about our situation. I really don't know what to think. I've never considered myself rich, and yet some people say we are quite wealthy."

Salomon didn't answer.

"And others say there are no savings."

"They're both right," he replied.

"Ah, I see. We would be wealthy if it weren't for the loans. That's why there are no savings." She threw her arms around him. "You're just too good, too kind."

He looked annoyed. "The War of Independence is not a charity. It's an investment."

"But you know that you'll never get paid back."

He took her hand and kissed it. "Don't worry your pretty head. I saw a bolt of blue velvet on the dock today. I think I'll buy it for you and you'll have a new dress. And if you will only stop worrying about my health, I'll bring you a fan and some French perfume."

"But Haym, our children—will there be something left for them to inherit from us?"

"Yes, a country where they'll be free to differ in the way they worship God and still enjoy the friendship of other people. I want most to leave the children an opportunity for happiness equal to that of the other citizens of a new nation and a feeling that they are as important a part of the new nation as anyone else."

Rachel couldn't argue with the man she respected and loved so much. She recognized the truth in what he said. Opportunity was a far more valuable legacy than dollars.

twelve

Robert Morris refrained from contacting Salomon for a long time after the Yom Kippur plea, even though his need for funds continued to be desperate. A comment by the king of England traveled across the Atlantic Ocean: "My one true ally," he had said, "is the rebels' money—or their lack of it."

King George knew Congress in America had no gold or silver, the basic money of the world, to back up the paper dollars they were issuing. All thirteen colonies (each with paper money of its own) were better off financially than the central government and wouldn't accept Continental bills at face value.

As a result, by 1780 a Philadelphia housewife had to take thousands of Continental dollars to market with her. A frying pan cost $125, boots $600, a fork $37, a clock $1,000. And some shopkeepers refused to accept Continental dollars at all. Maimed and destitute veterans clamored for food and clothing and rioted when they found that their pay was worth almost nothing. They dragged certain shopkeepers who would not accept the paper money to the riverbank, to be hung or shot as "enemies of the Revolution."

Alexander Hamilton, an aide to George Washington, dispatched a message to Robert Morris supporting what Morris had said all along: "It is by restoring public credit, not by gaining battles, that we are finally to gain our object." For a brief period in 1778, when France first became America's ally, Morris had dared to hope the French loans would save America from bankruptcy. But in the next two years, to his despair, with French troops in New Jersey and Rhode Island and a French minister residing in Philadelphia, French army bills had flooded the market and lost their value, as wild speculation took place and brokers undersold each other.

Haym Salomon explained it all to McRae. "Whether or not America can continue fighting depends now on the Office of Finance getting top dollar for those French bills. The source of the wildcat bills is the paymaster-general of the French army. Just like us, the French can't buy anything until they convert the bills into cash. A French officer in America cares

In this French loan note Haym Salomon's name is spelled Solomons.

little about keeping up the value of his bills here. He knows that his mother country is rich, and therefore he is not worried about her. What worries him is how to lay his hands on some ready cash."

"What does that have to do with us?"

"The market must be dependable and stabilized," Salomon said firmly. "And I propose to do it."

"How?"

"After gathering all the French army's bills that I can, I'll persuade the French minister—"

"How do you expect to get to him?" McRae interrupted. "He's never heard of you."

"Buying up the bills should attract his attention," explained Salomon. "And when I see him I hope to convince him that all French bills of exchange should be sold through one man, who would endorse them and never undersell. That would give all the French bills a standard value."

"You would be the endorser?"

"Yes."

"But suppose the Revolution fails? The endorser would be ruined."

"The Revolution will not fail!" Salomon said fiercely.

Soon after this conversation, an ad appeared in the *Pennsylvania Journal.*

A FEW BILLS *of* EXCHANGE *on* FRANCE, ST. EUSTATIA & AMSTERDAM, *To Be Sold By* HAYM SALOMON, *Broker*

The said Salomon will attend every day at the coffee-house between the hours of twelve and two, where he may be met with, and any kind of business in the brokerage will be undertaken by him; and those gentlemen who choose to favor him with their business may depend on the greatest care and punctuality.

The coffeehouse crowd was puzzled. Why would Salomon be buying up French bills for more money than anyone had paid in a long while and putting his very reliable signature on them? Was this some kind of Jewish trick?

Several weeks later a messenger delivered the compliments of the French minister, Chevalier de la Luzerne, who requested the honor of a visit from Monsieur Salomon.

Salomon promptly called on the French minister.

"Mr. Salomon," the French minister began in halting English, "for months American brokers have complained that no one wants to buy French bills of exchange at a fair price. Now I hear that you are offering those brokers even more than they ask. Why are you doing France this favor?"

Haym picked up the conversation in French. "If you excuse my saying so, sir, your army bills were bringing a low price because of ignorant handling. For the good of the American Revolution, French bills of exchange must be sold at face value. The new government needs every cent."

"Ah, now I see," Luzerne said. "Incredible! You are trying to stabilize the market with your good name."

"Nothing is more important to me than the success of the Revolution."

"And you are a Jew?"

"I am."

"I've asked Robert Morris, 'Who is this Haym Salomon? Is he honest?' And he says, 'Yes, I've checked. It seems he is an honest man.' And I say, 'Then why don't you employ this able man to help you? You need assistance so desperately.' And he will not answer."

Haym remained silent.

"I have no feelings about Jews one way or another. What speaks to me in a man is not what he says he believes, but what he does! Morris is trapped by prejudice."

Salomon sat quietly, overwhelmed by the words of the outspoken French aristocrat.

"Mr. Salomon. It occurs to me that you in your little office on Front Street are doing for the nation's credit what Washington is doing on the battlefield for the people's independence. With your permission, from now on, monies of the French army in America will pass through you. All bills will be endorsed and sold by you. I'm so glad that along with your other talents you speak French. It will make our dealings much easier. I shall advise Robert Morris of my decision in the morning."

"Thank you, Your Excellency."

"*We* are the ones who are grateful."

A few days later Robert Morris was officially appointed superintendent of finance of the American government. And Salomon received a note saying,

If Mr. Haym Salomon will call upon Mr. Robert Morris tomorrow at 3:00 such business may be concluded which will be to their advantage and to the advantage of their country.

thirteen

Robert Morris sat behind a polished mahogany desk. He was a big man in his late forties, to judge by his substantial paunch. Haym had been told by a fashionable Philadelphia artist who had painted Morris's portrait that he'd seen a smile on this haughty person's face only once. That was when he heard that his ship had come safely into port with British spoils. Now the Jewish broker sat watching

Philadelphia's financial expert pore over a letter from the French minister, de la Luzerne.

"Mr. Salomon," Morris finally began in a cold voice, "you must know that Congress had officially conferred on me the title of superintendent of finance."

"My congratulations, sir."

"Having the official title unfortunately does not make my job easier. Now we are more desperate than ever for money to finance the Revolution!"

"I know that."

"Luzerne informs me that he wants you to handle all the bills of exchange issued to the French in America. He says here you do not intend to make a profit on your services. I don't know any businessman in America who's not looking for profit. What is your motive then?"

Salomon controlled his anger. "The same motive I had when I raised money that you needed for General Washington from some Jewish citizens praying on their holiest day."

"The situation was desperate or I wouldn't have come to you."

"So you stated in your note that day. My motive is patriotic. From the beginning I've risked all for independence. No one has ever accused *me* of Tory leanings."

Morris's eyes narrowed. He was still called a Tory by some in the coffeehouses and he knew it. Immediately Haym regretted wounding him. Though Robert Morris held out against the Declaration of Independence in '76, no one could ignore his contribution to the cause since then.

The official smoothed a sheet of paper on his desk and studied it a few moments. Finally he said, "How good is your credit?"

"No one has ever refused to accept my signature."

Morris nodded. "Just what my information here tells me."

"I believe I could handle all sorts of bills of exchange to the advantage of the Treasury if they were entrusted to me."

"And what commission would you ask to be paid for your work? Two percent is the current rate."

"No fee."

"Mr. Salomon!" Robert Morris spat out the words. "I find it hard enough just to do business with a—with a—Hebrew! To deal with a fanatic would be impossible!"

"Well then, let us agree to one quarter of one percent commission."

"Agreed. Now I am about to leave for the encampment at Westchester. General Washington begged me to come quickly. He hinted that a demand will come out of the meeting for a sum larger than any we've been asked for before. At all costs we'll have to fill that demand."

"You can depend on me." Salomon said firmly.

The victory by George Washington's forces at Monmouth in 1778 had done little to end the war. The British army was so superior and so far outnumbered the Americans that Washington could not find a second opportunity to risk a full-scale battle that would decide the war. Months of skirmishes and minor attacks and counterattacks stretched into years. Time was working in favor of the British. The wealth of an empire stood behind them. Washington must plan for a strong offensive—and quickly.

In the summer of 1780 Washington received word that the French general Rochambeau, with some six thousand first-rate, fully equipped regular soldiers, had landed in Newport, Rhode Island, and awaited his orders. Jubilantly, the American commander rode north to meet Rochambeau in Connecticut, where the two outlined important strategy.

Because there were two main bodies of British troops in the Colonies, one based in New York City and the other in the south under Cornwallis, the American army had to be maintained in two parts. The recently appointed General Greene commanded the army in Virginia and George Washington the one in Westchester County, New York.

Washington badly wanted to take New York City. But he realized that even if he combined his troops with Rochambeau's, it was doubtful if they would have the force to take New York from the well-fed, well-equipped Hessians, who were dug in behind strong defenses. Instead, he decided, he would steal out of camp and march the combined French and American troops five hundred miles south to Virginia, to join General Greene in a surprise full-scale battle against Cornwallis.

In the meantime the French fleet, under Admiral de Grasse, would sail from its base in the West Indies. The fleet would keep supplies from reaching the British army and close off escape by sea.

To carry out this campaign, Washington told Robert Morris he would need a large sum of money.

"Of course," Morris replied testily, "everything takes money, but there is none right now."

"You must raise it somehow."

" 'Somehow' is how I've been raising funds up to now."

"Could you appeal again to the states to share the burden?"

Morris shook his head. "Each state waits to see what the other will do before it makes a move. Jealousy between them makes a reliable revenue impossible. Actually, it's a miracle that foreign governments give us aid when they see that none is forthcoming at home."

Washington crossed the meeting room of his headquarters to a map of the Colonies hanging on the wall. He no longer seemed to be listening to Robert Morris. A new thought seemed to have crossed his mind.

"If you could hold off until the fall, general—" Morris began.

"Impossible."

"We can't turn out another issue of paper money right now. But in the fall—"

"Things will be different?"

"Spain or France might give us another loan."

"Yes, France . . . ," Washington mused. With his finger, he traced a line to Rhode Island and drew a circle around the area in which the French general Rochambeau and his men were encamped.

fourteen

In Philadelphia, confidence in the Revolution fell to its lowest point. While the superintendent of finance was away, his assistant, Governeur Morris, was in charge of finances. (He was not related to Robert, even though they had the same last name.) The assistant made unreasonable demands on Salomon's energy and capabilities. He would insist that Haym sell bills of exchange at a moment's notice and would send around every congressman who could no longer afford a meal, maimed and incapacitated soldiers who deserved pensions, and urgent requests for barrels of flour and cornmeal.

Salomon would seek out merchants on the docks as they contracted for newly arrived cargoes, and he would beg for supplies. Other times he'd corner a fellow member of Mikveh Israel and talk him into a new donation to the government. His friends began to avoid him; his health broke under the strain.

When Robert Morris returned to the city, he found a steady stream of money trickling into the Treasury. Salomon was selling the government bills of exchange at prices it had never been able to get before. Then word reached the Office of Finance that Washington had met with Rochambeau. The Frenchman, convinced that the combined armies should march south immediately, offered him half the French military chest—$40,000. The campaign could begin.

Spain also granted America a loan. And the king's agent, Don Francisco de Rendón, ordered that Haym Salomon, not Robert Morris, be consulted as to how the Spanish bills of exchange should be handled.

Robert Morris resented the suggestion, suspecting it was a criticism of his own ability to handle a loan. He summoned Salomon.

"Are you acquainted with the Spanish king's agent, Don Francisco de Rendón?" Morris asked.

"Yes," answered Salomon, "he's been having trouble maintaining himself here in the style which he feels his position demands. I've helped him in any way that I could."

"I see. Then he made his request because he was grateful to you, I suppose. Well, at his order you are to be consulted on the sale of the Spanish bills of exchange."

That evening Robert Morris wrote in his diary;

June 8, 1781, Congress having assigned the management of the monies granted by His Most Christian Majesty to assist in a vigorous prosecution of the present campaign to the superintendent of finance, I agreed with Mr. Haym Salomon the broker, who has been employed by the officers of His Most Christian Majesty to make sale of their army and navy bills.... I am to draw for the monies granted as aforesaid. His brokerage to be settled hereafter.

In a letter to the governor of Havana, Don Francisco de Rendón wrote about his trials in America. He stated that if it had not been for the assistance of Haym Salomon when Spain was in secret alliance with the Revolutionary government, and all supplies were cut off by British cruisers, His Majesty's mission would not have been maintained.

Not long after the Spanish loan, Morris confided to Salomon that General Washington had embarked on a secret and crucial campaign which would need financing.

Once more Haym visited merchants' stores, coffeehouses, the homes of friends. He haunted the docks. Money was impossible to get. His life became a nightmare of seeking. His assistant called him a fool, his wife wept at the sight of him. He came home each night weary and haggard, and his cough got worse and worse. His enemies at the coffeehouses ridiculed him. Still he drove himself to fulfill his pledge.

More and more frequently the entries in Morris's diary recorded visits and conferences with Salomon. Morris also confided in his diary that he could hardly eat or sleep once Washington started his long march south.

As the combined force of American and French troops marched to Virginia, the French fleet was sailing toward the British ships in the Chesapeake Bay. De Grasse's thrust would keep the English ships from supplying Cornwallis.

Under the combined attack by the Revolutionary forces on land and sea, Cornwallis was able to hold out only for three weeks. On October 17, 1781, he asked for surrender terms and on October 19 he surrendered at Yorktown. It was a decisive victory for the Americans.

Loud voices in Parliament in London spoke out against continuing the war with America, which had already dragged on for six years. These protests, however, brought no immediate results. With British garrisons still in Charleston and Savannah and sympathizers in all the Colonies, why give up?

Now new problems troubled General Washington. The war went on, but old campaigners had to be furloughed, and many of his officers who suffered bad health handed in their resignations. Where would he find replacements for these men? Enlistments were hard to obtain at this time. He could promote some of the deserving officers who remained, but could he stand the jealous squabbling about rank that would result—the hearings he would have to grant to people who were dissatisfied, the disgraceful messages with petty grievances that would fly over his head to the Congress? Bear it he must.

He made "Mad Anthony" Wayne the leader in the South, and he himself led his men north to Newburgh, New York. Robert Morris groaned when he heard the news. An army in the north again, with winter coming! Where would the money for supplies come from?

"Ross," he barked, "find Mr. Haym Salomon!" He was to repeat this order many times in the next seven months:

November 12, Sent for Salomon and gave him orders....

March 19, 1782, Mr. H. Salomon the broker came to negotiate about the bills....

March 25, Mr. Haym Salomon the broker came to inform me that bills of exchange would be wanted this week. I shall want money....

On July 12, 1782, Haym Salomon asked Morris's permission to publish the fact that he was broker to the Office of Finance. He felt it would help raise money. The request was granted and Morris wrote in his diary:

This broker has been useful to the public interest.... I have consented as I do not see that any disadvantage can possibly arise to the public service but the reverse.

Salomon managed to raise money that summer but there always seemed to be an emergency. When the French cut off their funds to America, he could no longer earn anything on their bills of exchange. On August 28 Morris wrote:

Salomon the broker came and I urged him to leave no stone unturned to find out money and the means by which I can obtain it.

It seemed to Haym that almost every possibility to raise funds had been exhausted. Finally there was no other choice: the Treasury had to go into business as a trader of goods to try to earn the needed money. Haym haunted the docks and warehouses, buying and selling at a profit.

In his diary Robert Morris spelled Haym Salomon's name as Solomon.

He placed the following ad in the *Freeman's Journal:*

H A Y M   S A L O M O N
Broker to the Office of Finance,

to the consul general of France, and to the treasurer of the French army, at his office in Front Street between Market and Arch Streets, buys and sells on commission.

Bank stock, bills of exchange on France, Spain, Holland, and other parts of Europe and the West Indies, and inland bills at the usual commission. He buys and sells Loan Office certificates, Continental and state money, of this or any other state, paymaster . . . [or] paper transactions (bills of exchange excepted) he will charge his employers no more than one half percent for his commission.

He procures money on loan for short time and gets notes and bills discounted.

Gentlemen and others residing in this state or any of the United States, by sending their orders to this office, may depend on having their business transacted with as much fidelity and expedition as if they were themselves present.

He receives tobacco, sugars, tea, and every other sort of goods to sell on commission; for which purpose he has provided proper stores.

He flatters himself, his assiduity, punctuality, and extensive connections in his business, as a broker, is well established in various parts of Europe and in the United States in particular.

All persons who shall please to favor him with their business may depend upon his utmost exertion for their interest, and part of the money advanced, if desired.

fifteen

To ease the nation's financial problem, Morris had proposed a national Bank of North America in 1781. The Treasury had little to offer the bank in the way of capital so Morris turned to France for money. The French, however, still feared that the British might win the war, and they sent the bank only a small part of the expected loan. Morris then approached individual depositors. By this time Haym Salomon's once-considerable fortune had dwindled to only $900.

He used the sum to become a stockholder and the principal depositor in the Bank of North America.

In spite of bad health, Salomon continued to work long, hard hours. He felt old and tired at the age of forty-one, and finally suffered a hemorrhage which forced him to stay in bed. All through his sickness Rachel sat at his bedside, keeping herself busy with needlework. Ezekiel, Sallie, and the latest addition to the family, baby Deborah, played before the fireplace.

Haym, propped high on pillows, studied his children. He realized sadly that he scarcely knew them, so busy had he been with the "more important" business of the government.

While he was recovering from his illness his friends Barnard Gratz and Isaac Moses came to see him. Knowing the seriousness of his illness, they found it hard to make conversation.

"I hear you joined the Masons," Gratz commented during one visit.

"Yes, the Solomon Lodge Number Two."

"Solomon as in King Solomon?" joked Moses. "Or Salomon as in Haym?"

"As in King," said Salomon.

"Haym, we are concerned about the constitution of Pennsylvania as it affects Jews and are planning to register a protest," Gratz said. "We discovered that while people seeking work as state employees don't have to pass a test in religion in order to qualify, they *are* compelled to take an oath that they believe in both the Hebrew Bible and the New Testament when they assume office. We would like to write a letter to the Pennsylvania Council of Censors, because this condition would mean that a Jew could never hold office with the government. This is no way for a new country to begin. We must protest now!"

"Our petition will ask that this practice be abolished," said Moses.

"I will be happy to sign my name," Salomon said.

"Now, my friend," confided Barnard Gratz, "we have good news to pass on to you. We now have so many people at services on the Sabbath that we overflow the Cauffman house. New trustees have been elected."

"Who are they?"

"Hayman Levy, Jonas Phillips, Benjamin Seixas, Simon Nathan, and myself."

Isaac Moses put in proudly, "They elected me president."

"Congratulations, Isaac."

"And we all voted to build a synagogue to house Congregation Mikveh Israel."

Salomon's jaw dropped. "Build in the middle of a war?"

"Of course we must plan first."

"Everyone is enthusiastic. Not one vote against the proposal," said Gratz.

"But how will you raise the money to build? Everybody has been terribly affected by the war. If there's an extra dollar left in the Jewish community I'd like to know about it." He fell back against his pillows. "You are businessmen. I don't have to tell you what conditions are."

"Yes, we know the conditions," Isaac Moses said. "But, Haym, we are looking beyond the present. We believe independence will be won and that Philadelphia will be the capital of this new country of ours. Think of that! Wouldn't you expect a capital city with over one thousand Jews to have a worthy synagogue?"

"I repeat, how will you pay for it? A third of the thousand Jews lost everything when they fled the British and came here. They have nothing left to give you."

"We don't need much to start building. And when the war is over we'll collect the money we loaned to the delegates to Congress and—"

Salomon smiled sadly. "Don't expect to be repaid."

"In addition," said Moses, ignoring Haym's warning, "we are going to send an appeal for money to other Jewish communities—Rhode Island, Lancaster, Cape Francis, the Virgin Islands, and Surinam."

Haym caught a bit of their enthusiasm. "I'd like to contribute," he said. He knew there was not one dollar in his bank account. But if he could get back on his feet and go to the coffeehouse something profitable might turn up. "Please record my name as pledging three hundred pounds!"

A few weeks later Haym Salomon received word that a privateer with a rich cargo had come into port. His profits would cover his synagogue pledge. He thanked God and found the strength to get out of bed and walk to Third and Cherry Streets to see where the new house of worship was going to be built. Just think, a synagogue in Philadelphia, Mikveh Israel—Hope of Israel.

The war dragged to an end on April 11, 1783. Congress issued a proclamation and all the bells in Philadelphia pealed forth. That night people lit bonfires and danced in the streets. From their parlor window the Salomon children clapped their hands at the magical sight of the lighted ships in the Delaware and the fireworks bursting into flower high over the glistening water.

"It's all over, Haym," McRae said jubilantly. "Now we can think of our business and start to build it up again."

"Now maybe I can think of my wife and children," said Salomon.

"Now maybe you'll think of *yourself*," Rachel ordered.

But the superintendent of finance still called for the help of the broker. "The men are coming home now." he said. "They'll be pouring into town, rioting for their back pay. We've got to have money!"

And Salomon struggled to raise it, using up his remaining strength.

In September 1783 the treaty of peace was formally signed in Paris. A month later George Washington gave his farewell address to the army, and in December he resigned his commission as commander in chief. Not till then did Morris tell Salomon the pressure was finally over and he could rest. On the day of their last negotiation, the two men shook hands. The expression on Robert Morris's face was one of deep respect for the Jewish broker he had once scorned.

sixteen

In February 1784 Haym Salomon fell ill again and was forced to rest in bed. Rabbi Seixas visited him often. Next to the vigorous, young-looking man, Haym had the appearance of a corpse, though he was only five years older. His eyes were sunken and his ears protruded. It took a great effort for him to speak.

"I don't want to tire you unnecessarily, Haym," the rabbi said one day. "I really came to say goodbye.

I'm leaving Philadelphia. My original New York pulpit has called me back."

"When do you leave?"

"In a month."

"How will we ever find a replacement for you?"

Salomon closed his eyes.

"I'm sure you'll find a fine rabbi. But I can't leave without thanking you for the privilege of your friendship. Your example has taught me very much."

"Taught the rabbi?"

"Yes, you taught me to interest myself in all kinds of people and to invest myself in events."

"I may go to New York myself. With that good harbor, there will be great opportunities there. I think I'll open an office there as soon as this weak spell is over."

In 1784 Haym Salomon placed a long advertisement in various newspapers. Part of it read:

H A Y M   S A L O M O N
Broker to the Office of Finance,

having procured a license for the exercising the employment of an auctioneer in the city of New York, has now opened for the reception of every species of merchandise, his house No. 22 Wall Street, lately occupied by Mr. Anthony L. Bleeker (one of the best stands in that city) and every branch of business which in the smallest degree appertains to the

professions of factor, auctioneer, and broker will be
transacted in it, with that fidelity, dispatch, and punctuality which has hitherto characterized his dealings.

Salomon worked hard on his plans for the new
business with his partner, Jacob Mordecai. As 1784
drew to a close he suffered another hemorrhage and
was confined to bed once more.

"But I can't afford to rest now," he told his wife.

"Let me spoil you like a little boy," said Rachel.

"It's you who should be pampered. I feel so bad
that our funds are low now, just when the new baby
is expected. I want him to have all the things his
brother and sisters have had."

"You're sure it will be a boy."

"Yes, it will be a boy," Haym insisted. "Your
birthday is next month. I'd like to get my twenty-two-
year-old wife something to delight her—something
luxurious. As soon as this weakness passes, you'll see,
everyone will be taken care of. I'll pay my debts and
build a nice savings account in the bank for you and the
children."

But Salomon did not recover his strength. He
remained in bed. Rachel sat beside him, and his children played around him. Little by little his vitality
slipped away.

Five days into the new year of 1785, at the age of
forty-five, the man who stood behind Robert Morris
and produced the actual money which kept the Revo-

lution going, the patriot who never sought the lime-
light, never wore a uniform or flourished a sword, but
who performed an enormous service for his country,
died.

His obituary appeared in the *Pennsylvania Packet.*

DIED, HAYM SALOMON,

after a lingering illness. An eminent broker of this
city, he was a native of Poland and of the Hebrew
nation. He was remarkable for his skill and integrity
in his profession and for his generous and humane
deportment.

The *Pennsylvania Journal* of January 8, 1785, said
only:

On Thursday, died Haym Salomon, a broker.

Rachel Salomon bore her fourth child three months after her husband's death. She named the baby Haym M. Salomon. The young widow inherited $358,000—but only in the form of notes showing that various people owed her money and in greatly depreciated government currency. She was unable to collect on the big personal loans Haym had made to the Spanish ambassador and Robert Morris and others. Since she knew little about her husband's business affairs or the handling of money, at the request of the state treasurer of Pennsylvania, she turned over to him all her securities and certificates.

Months later, desperately in need of support, she still had received no money. She wrote to the treasurer repeatedly, but her letters were ignored. Finally, after a long delay, the treasurer's office reported that all the papers regarding her inheritance had been "lost."

Eventually Rachel Salomon found security in remarriage, this time to David Heilbrun of New York City.

When he grew up, Ezekiel Salomon served as a purser in the United States Navy and became a cashier of the New Orleans branch of the United States Bank. Sallie married Joseph Andrews of New York in 1794, and Deborah married Simon Myers Cohen in 1801.

Haym M. Salomon, the son who never knew his father, put aside his career as a merchant in 1844 in order to gather evidence to prove his father's claim against the government. He devoted all his energies to recovering the family's rightful inheritance.

As evidence, Haym M. Salomon offered the sworn statement of Robert Morris, taken in 1805 when he himself was in jail for debt, that no payment to Salomon appeared in his private accounts and that none had been made by the Treasury to Salomon or his heirs. He also presented other documents, one of them a letter from James Madison, a member of Congress when Salomon knew him and later the president of the United States for two terms. The letter, written in 1783, told about Haym Salomon's contributions to the government.

The Thirtieth, Thirty-first, Thirty-second, and

The monument in Chicago erected to Haym Salomon (left), George Washington, and Robert Morris.

Thirty-eight Congresses favored paying the debt, and the Sixty-ninth Congress recommended payment to the heirs, but the recommendation never passed both houses.

Presidents Theodore Roosevelt, William H. Taft, Woodrow Wilson, Calvin Coolidge, Herbert Hoover, and Franklin Delano Roosevelt all paid tribute to the patriot's memory. A monument was erected in Chicago on December 15, 1941, as a joint memorial to George Washington, Robert Morris, and Haym Salomon. William Salomon, Haym's great-grandson, gave $2,500 as the first contribution toward the statue.

Carved into the base of the monument are these words of President George Washington, written in 1790:

THE GOVERNMENT OF THE UNITED STATES WHICH GIVES TO BIGOTRY NO SANCTION, TO PER-SECUTION NO ASSISTANCE, REQUIRES ONLY THAT THEY WHO LIVE UNDER ITS PROTECTION SHOULD DEMEAN THEMSELVES AS GOOD CITIZENS IN GIV-ING IT ON ALL OCCASIONS THEIR EFFECTUAL SUP-PORT.

In 1975, in preparation for the two-hundredth anniversary of American independence, the United States

Postal Service issued a series of stamps commemorating "Contributors to the Cause" of the American Revolution. Among the heroes so honored was—Haym Salomon. His citation reads:

BUSINESSMAN AND BROKER HAYM SALOMON WAS RESPONSIBLE FOR RAISING MOST OF THE MONEY NEEDED TO FINANCE THE AMERICAN REVOLUTION AND LATER TO SAVE THE NEW NATION FROM COLLAPSE.

Thus a grateful nation remembers one of its devoted sons—who made freedom his cause.

SHIRLEY MILGRIM, a native of Philadelphia, is the author of *Stories of Courage,* a collection of five biographies for young readers, and *Pathways to Independence* (with illustrations by Richard Fish), a historical guide to Independence National Park and surrounding areas. She has also written five dramas that have been produced on television.

RICHARD FISH is a celebrated artist and designer who makes his home in Havertown, Pennsylvania. In addition to his work on *Pathways to Independence,* he has illustrated the highly acclaimed *Exploring Old Cape Cod.*